Christmas
Navidad

Josie Keogh

Traducción al español:
Eduardo Alamán

PowerKiDS
press™

New York

Published in 2013 by The Rosen Publishing Group, Inc.
29 East 21st Street, New York, NY 10010

First Edition

Editor: Amelie von Zumbusch
Book Design: Andrew Povolny   Traducción al español: Eduardo Alamán

Photo Credits: Cover Altrendo Images/Getty Images; p. 5 Gary John Norman/Taxi/Getty Images; p. 7 Comstock Images/Thinkstock; p. 9 Altrendo Images/Stockbyte/Getty Images; pp. 11, 19, 23 iStockphoto/Thinkstock; p. 13 Monkey Business/Thinkstock; p. 15 Boston Globe/Getty Images; p. 17 Vstock LLC/Getty Images; p. 21 Johnnie Pakington/Flickr/Getty Images.

Library of Congress Cataloging-in-Publication Data

Keogh, Josie.
 Christmas = Navidad / by Josie Keogh ; translated by Eduardo Alamán. — 1st ed.
   p. cm. — (Powerkids readers: happy holidays! / ¡felices fiestas!)
 Includes index.
 ISBN 978-1-4488-9968-5 (library binding)
 1. Christmas—Juvenile literature. I. Alamán, Eduardo. II. Title.
 GT4985.5.K47 2013
 394.2663—dc23
                                        2012022323

Websites: Due to the changing nature of Internet links, PowerKids Press has developed an online list of websites related to the subject of this book. This site is updated regularly. Please use this link to access the list: www.powerkidslinks.com/pkrhh/xmas/

Manufactured in the United States of America

CPSIA Compliance Information: Batch #W13PK3: For Further Information contact Rosen Publishing, New York, New York at 1-800-237-9932

Contents

Contenido

Christmas is fun!

¡La Navidad es divertida!

You can meet **Santa**.

Puedes conocer a **Santa**.

A baby **reindeer** is a calf.

El bebé de un **reno** es su cría.

9

People send cards.

La gente envía tarjetas
de Navidad.

11

They make treats.

———————————————

Se hacen convites.

They sing songs.

Se cantan canciones.

"Jingle Bells" was once a Thanksgiving song.

"Jingle Bells" comenzó como una canción del Día de Acción de Gracias.

16

Yule log cakes are from France.

En Francia se preparan **pasteles en forma de troncos**.

18

19

Christmas trees began
in Germany.

Los árboles de Navidad
comenzaron en Alemania.

Firs and pines are the top kinds.

Los abetos y los pinos son los árboles de Navidad más comunes.

23

WORDS TO KNOW / PALABRAS QUE DEBES SABER

reindeer

(el) reno

Santa

Santa

Yule log

(el) pastel en
forma de tronco